WORLD LEADERS

JACINDA ARDERN

PRIME MINISTER OF NEW ZEALAND

by Cynthia Kennedy Henzel

FOCUS READERS

www.focusreaders.com

Focus Readers is distributed by North Star Editions:
sales@northstareditions.com | 888-417-0195

Produced for Focus Readers by Red Line Editorial.

Content Consultant: Jennifer Curtin, Professor of Politics and International Relations, University of Auckland

Photographs ©: KYDPL Kyodo/Kyodo/AP Images, cover, 1; photocosmos1/Shutterstock Images, 4–5; Red Line Editorial, 7, 27 (right); Nick Perry/AP Images, 9, 11, 36–37, 42–43; Ruth Lawton/Shutterstock Images, 12–13; riekephotos/Shutterstock Images, 15; Admirari/Shutterstock Images, 17; Lukasz Stefanski/Shutterstock Images, 19; Wendy_Paul/iStockphoto, 20–21; Simon Baker/Reuters/Newscom, 23; David White/Rex Features, 24–25; Rainer Lesniewski/Shutterstock Images, 27 (left), 27 (center); Jason Oxenham/Getty Images News/Getty Images, 29; Mark Baker/AP Images, 30–31, 38; Dmitri Ogleznev/ Shutterstock Images, 32; Shirley Kwok/Pacific Press/Newscom, 35; greg0070/iStockphoto, 41; Retropix/ Splash News/Newscom, 45

Library of Congress Cataloging-in-Publication Data
Names: Henzel, Cynthia Kennedy, 1954- author.
Title: Jacinda Ardern : Prime Minister of New Zealand / by Cynthia Kennedy Henzel.
Description: Lake Elmo, MN : Focus Readers, [2019] | Series: World leaders | Audience: Grades 7-8. | Includes bibliographical references and index.
Identifiers: LCCN 2018040011 (print) | LCCN 2018041379 (ebook) | ISBN 9781641855358 (pdf) | ISBN 9781641854771 (ebook) | ISBN 9781641853613 (hardcover : alk. paper) | ISBN 9781641854191 (pbk. : alk. paper)
Subjects: LCSH: Ardern, Jacinda, 1980- | Prime ministers--New Zealand--Biography. | New Zealand--Politics and government--1972-
Classification: LCC DU420.34.A73 (ebook) | LCC DU420.34.A73 H46 2019 (print) | DDC 993.04/12--dc23
LC record available at https://lccn.loc.gov/2018040011

Printed in the United States of America
Mankato, MN
October, 2018

ABOUT THE AUTHOR

Cynthia Kennedy Henzel has a BS in social studies education and an MS in geography. She has worked as a teacher-educator in many countries. Currently, she writes books and develops education materials for social studies, history, science, and ELL students. She has written more than 80 books for young people.

TABLE OF CONTENTS

CHAPTER 1

JACINDAMANIA

On August 31, 2017, Jacinda Ardern took her place on stage. The first debate of the New Zealand election was about to begin. Her opponent, Bill English, led the National Party. He had 26 years of experience in government. Plus, he was currently serving as prime minister.

Ardern was only 37 years old. She had been the Labour Party's leader for only a month. Even so, she was quickly gaining support from voters.

Jacinda Ardern helped the Labour Party gain support with a campaign promising change.

People felt that she spoke about topics that concerned them, such as families and housing. Young people liked her youth and energy. Plus, her **feminist** views appealed to many women. In fact, after just one week with Ardern as its leader, Labour had begun to catch up to National in polls. The media called her rise in popularity "Jacindamania."

During the debate, English downplayed Ardern's popularity. He claimed that the buzz about her would soon settle down. Instead, he focused on the state of the economy under his leadership. In contrast, Ardern talked about poverty, climate change, and the high cost of education. No one, she said, should settle for the problems facing New Zealand.

On September 23, people around the country cast their votes. To control the government in

New Zealand, a party must win a majority of seats in Parliament, either on its own or by agreeing to work with another party. Neither Labour nor National had enough seats for a majority. Both won fewer than 61 of the 120 seats in Parliament. As a result, they needed to form coalitions by convincing other parties to join with them.

FORMING A MAJORITY

Five political parties won seats in New Zealand's Parliament in 2017.

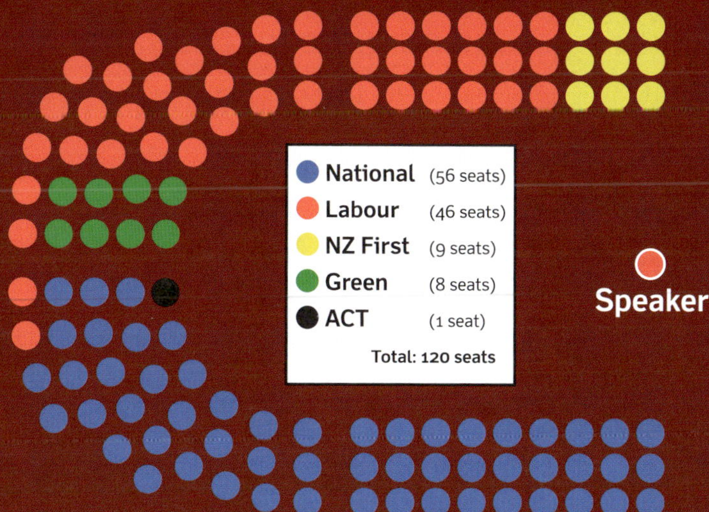

Because the Green Party had many ideas in common with Labour, people assumed the two parties would work together. But the Greens alone did not have enough seats to give Labour a majority. Ardern still needed another party to join her coalition. So, she approached Winston Peters, who led the New Zealand First Party.

Peters was quite different from Ardern. He had a gruff personality and **conservative** ideas. Even so, Ardern and Peters had some things in common. Like Ardern, Peters wanted New Zealand's government to do more for people who were struggling with poverty. He also wanted to support better jobs in rural parts of the country.

Ardern **negotiated** with Peters for weeks. So did Bill English. He tried to convince Peters to join with the National Party instead. Both English and Ardern waited for Peters to make his decision.

Winston Peters and Ardern sign an agreement to form a coalition.

On October 19, Peters announced that his party would join with Labour. Labour's coalition now had 63 seats, enough for a majority. That meant the Labour Party would control New Zealand's government. On October 25, Jacinda Ardern became the country's youngest prime minister in 150 years. In this new role, she would continue to make both change and headlines.

FOCUS ON
WINSTON PETERS

Winston Peters began serving in New Zealand's Parliament in 1979. At the time, he was a member of the National Party. But in 1993, Peters left National to form his own party, which he called New Zealand First.

New Zealand First holds a small number of seats in Parliament. But the party has a lot of power. It gets this power by forming coalitions. The larger National and Labour parties often need more seats to gain a majority in Parliament. These two parties try to make deals with Peters so his party will join their coalitions. His decision often determines which party will control Parliament.

The deals often give Peters a role in the new government. For instance, his deal with Ardern included his appointment as deputy prime minister. The deputy prime minister acts as the

In 2018, Peters was the longest-serving member in the New Zealand Parliament.

head of government when the prime minister is not available. Peters also serves as Ardern's foreign minister. In this role, he helps New Zealand work with other countries.

CHAPTER 2

AN ISLAND NATION

The country of New Zealand is a group of islands in the Pacific Ocean. It is located approximately 1,000 miles (1,600 km) east of Australia. The two main islands, North Island and South Island, are the largest. But New Zealand includes hundreds of smaller islands as well.

The country is known for its beautiful forests, mountains, and waterfalls. The land was first settled by the Maori between 1200 and 1300 CE.

New Zealand is made up of more than 500 islands.

For hundreds of years, the Maori were the only people on the islands. They lived in tribes ruled by chiefs. That began to change in 1769, when British explorer James Cook reached New Zealand. After Cook's writing about the islands was published, Europeans began traveling to New Zealand. By 1840, 2,000 British people had settled there. The United Kingdom began plans to make New Zealand a **colony**.

In 1840, British officials called a meeting of Maori chiefs. The two groups signed the Treaty of Waitangi. The treaty gave the Maori the right to organize themselves, protect their culture, and control their own resources. In return, the British promised to protect the Maori.

Later that year, New Zealand became a British colony. Settlers flocked to the colony, often claiming Maori land. By 1850, British settlers

The Treaty of Waitangi still applies to the government's partnership with the Maori people today.

outnumbered the Maori living in New Zealand. Tension between the groups rose until 1860, when fighting broke out. Most of the fighting had ended by 1870, but the loss of land continued. By 1900, much Maori land had been taken by beef and dairy farmers.

By the early 1900s, the United Kingdom had begun allowing its colonies more freedom. New Zealand gradually gained more power to govern itself before becoming fully independent in 1947.

Even after becoming independent, New Zealand's government maintained ties to the United Kingdom. The British monarch is New Zealand's official head of state. However, the monarch does not play much of a role in the country's government. The actual work of government in New Zealand is done through Parliament.

Parliament has just one house, known as the House of Representatives. New Zealand holds elections to select members of Parliament (MPs) every three years. During an election, all voters cast two votes. The first vote is for the MP they want to represent their **district**. Seventy-one of the 120 seats in Parliament are filled by votes for these MPs.

The second vote is for the political party that they want to run the government. Parliament's 49 remaining seats are divided among the

The House of Representatives meets in Wellington, New Zealand's capital.

political parties, depending on how many votes each party receives. Each party makes a list of the people who will take its seats. The MPs given these seats are called List members.

After each election, the party that leads the coalition forms a cabinet. The cabinet includes approximately 20 ministers. Along with the prime minister, these ministers make most of the decisions about how the country should be run.

FOCUS ON
NEW ZEALAND

New Zealand is a parliamentary democracy. The prime minister, cabinet, and Parliament work together to run the government and make the country's laws. New Zealand has three official languages: English, Maori, and Sign. It has no official religion.

In 2015, nearly 75 percent of New Zealand's population was of European descent. Fifteen percent identified as Maori. In the past, these two groups were often sharply divided. In recent years, however, that has started to change. Maori culture has begun to be celebrated by all New Zealanders. The country also has a growing Asian population.

In 2018, New Zealand had an estimated population of 4.7 million. Most people live on the country's two main islands, North Island and South Island. The country's capital is Wellington.

October 6, 1769: Captain James Cook sights New Zealand.

February 6, 1840: The Maori people sign the Treaty of Waitangi with the United Kingdom.

September 19, 1893: New Zealand becomes the first country to allow women to vote.

November 25, 1947: New Zealand becomes an independent country.

October 25, 2017: Jacinda Ardern becomes New Zealand's prime minister.

CHAPTER 3

MAKING A DIFFERENCE

Jacinda Ardern was born in Hamilton, New Zealand, in 1980. Her father was a police officer, and her mother worked in a school cafeteria. The Arderns belonged to the Mormon Church. As a result of its teachings, Jacinda developed a strong sense of right and wrong.

Jacinda attended school in the nearby town of Morrinsville. She was a good student and enjoyed participating in many school activities.

Hamilton, the city where Ardern was born, is located on New Zealand's North Island.

Among others, she took part in the student council, the school newspaper, and the debating team. After school, Jacinda helped her family grow apples and pears to make extra money.

From a young age, Jacinda spoke out for what she thought was right. For example, her high school's dress code required girls to wear skirts. Jacinda thought this rule was unfair. So, she worked to change it. She convinced school officials to change the dress code so girls could wear trousers.

While in high school, Jacinda grew interested in politics. She joined the Labour Party when she was 17 years old. Jacinda's aunt, Marie Ardern,

THINK ABOUT IT

Jacinda's aunt taught her about politics. What people or events have influenced your beliefs about government?

Part of helping with a campaign involves setting up and taking down signs for candidates.

had been a member of Labour for many years. She offered to teach Jacinda about politics. Jacinda visited her aunt in New Plymouth. There, Jacinda helped Labour MP Harry Duynhoven run for reelection. Jacinda became a volunteer coordinator for his **campaign**. She knocked on doors and asked people to vote for him.

It soon became clear that Jacinda had a knack for politics. Her work helped Duynhoven win the election. The next year, her classmates voted her most likely to become prime minister.

CHAPTER 4

A RAPID RISE

Jacinda Ardern began studying politics and public relations at the University of Waikato in 1999. While in college, Ardern decided to leave the Mormon Church. She did not agree with its opposition to same-sex marriage.

Ardern graduated in 2001 and got a job as a researcher. She began working for Labour MP Phil Goff but soon joined the staff of Helen Clark, who had just won a second term as prime minister.

Ardern's political experience in high school prepared her to study and work in politics.

Clark became Ardern's mentor. Her advice and policies helped shape Ardern's political career. For instance, both women supported keeping New Zealand free of nuclear weapons.

In New Zealand, many young adults choose to take a working holiday. During this time, they find a job in a foreign country. In 2005, Ardern traveled to the United Kingdom to work for Prime Minister Tony Blair. He was the young and popular leader of the British Labour Party. Ardern helped his government work with small businesses. Ardern had another opportunity to travel in 2007. She was elected president of the International Union of Socialist Youth. This group's goals included reducing poverty, improving education, and promoting equality for women. Group members came from more than 100 countries. As president, Ardern visited

Jordan, Israel, Algeria, China, and several other countries.

Ardern returned to New Zealand in 2008. The Labour Party had chosen her to run for a seat in her home district of Waikato. The district was conservative, so Ardern was not expected to win.

BECOMING AN MP

New Zealand has 71 electorates. Voters in each of these districts elect one MP.

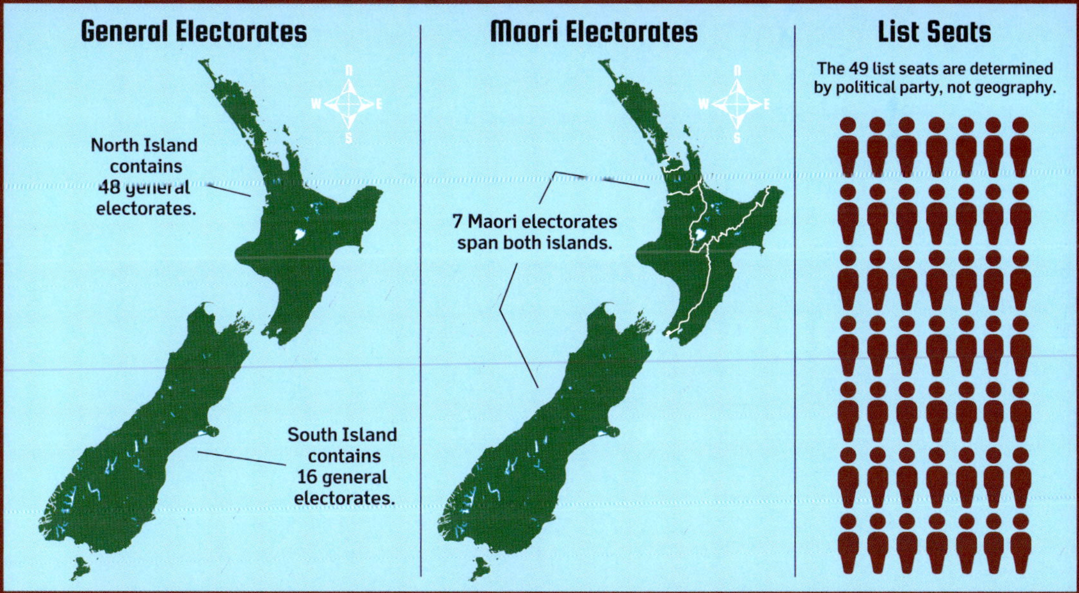

Indeed, she lost the election. But she received a seat in Parliament when the Labour Party selected her as a List MP.

At 28 years old, Ardern was now the youngest MP. She became spokesperson for Youth Affairs. This group works to create opportunities for New Zealand's young people. Ardern also served on the Justice Committee. She worked on issues related to crime, human rights, and voting.

Over the next few years, Ardern faced several setbacks. In 2011, she ran for a very competitive seat called Auckland Central. She did not win that seat, but she was again elected to be a List MP.

THINK ABOUT IT

Ardern visited several countries before working in Parliament. How might living in different countries be helpful for a career in politics?

As a young MP, Ardern rose quickly through the Labour Party's ranks.

During this second term, Ardern worked on two bills. One would allow same-sex couples to adopt children. The other would reduce child poverty. However, neither bill passed. Ardern lost the Auckland Central election again in 2014. Still, she remained a List MP.

Ardern's career began to take off in 2017. In February, she ran for the seat of a retiring MP and won by a large majority. And in March, she was chosen to be the deputy leader of the Labour Party. When Labour leader Andrew Little resigned in August, Ardern became the party's leader.

CHAPTER 5

FAMILIES FIRST

With less than two months until the 2017 election, Ardern began her campaign. At the time, many families in New Zealand were struggling. Wages were low. One-third of the country's children lived in poverty. New Zealand also had one of the highest rates of **domestic** violence in the developed world. A child in New Zealand went to the hospital every other day for injuries caused by family members or neglect.

Ardern speaks to workers at a factory in Christchurch, New Zealand.

More than half of homeless people in New Zealand live in the city of Auckland.

Housing was another big problem. New Zealand had a higher percentage of homeless people than any other wealthy country. Auckland, New Zealand's largest city, ranked fourth on a list of the world's most expensive places to buy a house. And the cost of houses was increasing more than 20 percent each year.

Even families who had houses often could not afford to heat them. New Zealand has mild temperatures near the coasts, where most people live. But temperatures in the winter can get as cold as 14 degrees Fahrenheit (–10°C). Each year, more than 1,000 people died because their houses were too cold. In addition, the country's rainy climate made many houses damp. Damp houses are harder to keep warm. They can also cause people to develop respiratory problems.

Ardern spoke to voters about these issues. She told them the Labour Party would provide money to help people pay for housing and heat. Ardern pointed out that young people often owed huge amounts of money after they finished college.

THINK ABOUT IT

What are the main challenges facing the country where you live? Can you think of any ways to solve them?

This debt made it even harder for them to buy houses. To solve this problem, Ardern said the government would help students pay for school.

Like her mentor Helen Clark, Ardern spoke about keeping New Zealand a nuclear-free zone. This meant the country would have no nuclear weapons. In addition to promoting peace, the policy would protect the environment from damages caused by nuclear testing.

New Zealand's environment plays a key role in the country's economy. Tourists come from around the world to admire New Zealand's mountains and rivers. In 2017, more than three million people visited New Zealand, making tourism one of the country's top industries.

However, huge dairy and farming businesses threatened the country's natural beauty. Large amounts of chemicals from fertilizers and

Ardern excelled at drawing crowds during her campaigns.

pesticides had washed into rivers and oceans. Ardern promised to repair this damage. She also supported efforts to slow climate change.

Ardern charmed voters with her openness and positive attitude. Huge crowds turned out to hear her speak. They also turned out at the polls, where their votes helped Ardern and the Labour Party win 46 seats in Parliament.

CHAPTER 6

ARDERN DELIVERS

After becoming prime minister in October, Ardern went straight to work. Within just a few months, she had helped create new programs and laws. Several focused on helping children and families. In December, for example, Parliament passed a Families Package. This law had several parts. It allowed parents to stay home from work for 22 weeks to care for new babies. In addition, it provided **aid** for poor children and their families.

Ardern focused on providing money for services to help families, children, and the poor.

Many of the changes Ardern's government made were focused on helping young people.

Another new law required the government to report on progress made in helping poor children.

Many New Zealanders could not afford the health care they needed. Costs had been rising for years. But Ardern's government worked to bring them down. It gave money to hospitals so children could get free checkups. It increased funding for **maternity** care and disability support. The government also provided aid to veterans who suffered from post-traumatic stress disorder, a mental illness that makes it difficult for people to hold jobs. Lawmakers hoped these changes would help more people have access to health care.

Other changes focused on decreasing family violence. For example, lawmakers hired 1,800 additional police officers to protect communities. Plus, they increased funding for services that helped families suffering from violence. Almost half of this money went to women's refuges, which are safe places where women and children can stay after fleeing violent homes.

The government began strategies to improve the housing crisis, too. One program would build 100,000 new homes in 10 years. Others helped families and elderly people pay their heating bills. And new laws required all rental homes to be warm and dry.

In addition to providing aid, Ardern focused on helping people earn more money. In 2017, women in New Zealand earned 9 percent less than men for doing the same jobs. This was down from 12 percent in 2015. But Ardern wanted to close the gap completely. She worked to provide equal pay for women. She also raised the **minimum wage**.

Ardern did not forget her promises to young people. In January 2018, New Zealand began a program to help its residents pay for higher education. The program paid for each student's first year of school. By 2024, the program aims to provide three years of free higher education.

Ardern also remembered her pledge to protect the environment. Under her leadership, MPs passed laws preventing gas and oil drilling along the country's coasts. Other goals focused on the future. The country pledged to have renewable

By banning oil drilling, Parliament hoped to reduce the risk of oil spills damaging New Zealand's coast.

electricity by 2035. By 2050, it aimed to have clean energy. That meant New Zealand would gradually stop using fuels, such as oil and coal, that contribute to global warming. Parliament created the Green Investment Fund to help industries that work with clean technology. Some of these goals will take years to achieve. But by the end of her first year in office, Ardern had made progress on most of her campaign promises.

CHAPTER 7

LOOKING AHEAD

Ardern has gained fame as an outspoken, **progressive** leader. For instance, during her campaign, a reporter asked if she planned to have children. He wondered if she could do the job of prime minister and have a family. Ardern told him that many women worked and raised families. She later said it was wrong for reporters to ask women this question. Many countries, including New Zealand, have laws against discrimination.

Ardern answers questions from reporters shortly after becoming Labour Party Leader.

A woman's job cannot depend on whether she will have children. Ardern's response made international news. Her words sparked a debate about women's roles at work and at home.

Ardern made headlines again in April 2018. She wore a feathered Maori cloak to a meeting for leaders of the British Commonwealth in London, England. By wearing the cloak, Ardern honored New Zealand's Maori heritage. She showed her desire to represent and respect the Maori people and their culture.

Two months later, Ardern's daughter was born. Ardern became the first elected leader to

THINK ABOUT IT

How are ideas about women and work different now than they were in the past? What do you think caused this change?

Ardern and her partner Clarke Gayford attend a dinner for Commonwealth leaders. Ardern is wearing a Maori cloak.

take a maternity leave while in office. After six weeks, Ardern resumed all her duties as prime minister. Her partner, Clarke Gayford, became a stay-at-home dad.

Jacindamania has continued long after the election. In June 2018, Ardern's approval rating remained at 76 percent. People continue to expect great things from the young prime minister and her campaign for change.

FOCUS ON

JACINDA ARDERN

Write your answers on a separate piece of paper.

1. Write a paragraph summarizing some of the main problems New Zealand faced during Ardern's 2017 campaign.

2. Does the area where you live tend to be progressive or conservative? Why do you think that is?

3. Which political party is Jacinda Ardern part of?

    A. Green Party
    B. Labour Party
    C. National Party

4. Why do people consider Ardern to be a progressive leader?

    A. Many of her policies involve making changes and social reform.
    B. Many of her policies do not involve changes to current systems.
    C. Many of her policies are related to businesses rather than families.

Answer key on page 48.

GLOSSARY

aid
Money the government gives to an organization or individual to help provide education, health care, or other services.

campaign
A series of activities such as traveling, speaking, or planning events to convince people to vote for a political candidate.

colony
An area of land that belongs to and is ruled by another country.

conservative
Supporting traditional views or values, often resisting changes.

district
A region that votes to elect a member of Parliament.

domestic
Taking place within a family or home.

feminist
Supporting equal rights for women and men.

maternity
Related to the period of time when a woman is pregnant, as well as shortly after she gives birth.

minimum wage
The lowest amount companies are allowed to pay employees.

negotiated
Held discussions to solve a problem or reach an agreement.

progressive
In favor of making changes or improvements, especially related to political or social issues.

TO LEARN MORE

BOOKS

Ganeri, Anita. *All About the Commonwealth.* London: Franklin Watts, 2016.

Smelt, Roselynn, Yong Jui Lin, and Joel Newsome. *New Zealand.* New York: Cavendish Square, 2018.

Walsh Shepherd, Donna. *New Zealand.* New York: Children's Press, 2016.

NOTE TO EDUCATORS

Visit **www.focusreaders.com** to find lesson plans, activities, links, and other resources related to this title.

INDEX

Answer Key: 1. Answers will vary; **2.** Answers will vary; **3.** B; **4.** A